CW01064548

Original title:
When Night Sings

Author: Zachary Prescott
ISBN HARDBACK: 978-9916-90-552-4
ISBN PAPERBACK: 978-9916-90-553-1

Symphony of the Hidden

In shadows deep, secrets play,
Whispers of night, in soft ballet.
Stars twinkle bright, a silent song,
Echoing dreams where shadows belong.

Moonlight glimmers on mystic streams,
Chasing the echoes of forgotten dreams.
Nature's pulse, a soft refrain,
In the hidden, love is gained.

The Night's Canvas Unfurled

The night unfolds like velvet skies,
With brushstrokes bright, where silence sighs.
Planets dance in a twinkling spree,
Woven whispers of what could be.

Each star a story waiting to tell,
In the depth of night, under its spell.
Colors swirl in the cosmic flow,
Painting a dream where wishes grow.

Seraphim of the Evening Sky

Angels glide on wings of light,
Dancing softly through the night.
Crimson hues merge with the dusk,
A sacred trust, a fragrant musk.

Celestial notes in harmony sing,
Caressing the air with each gentle fling.
Hearts entwined in the softest sigh,
Gaze in wonder at the evening sky.

Chords of the Nocturnal Breeze

The breeze carries songs from afar,
Cool and soft like a wishing star.
Each note a promise, a tender caress,
Whispered secrets in gentle finesse.

Murmurs of leaves in the moonlit dance,
Embraced by shadows, lost in romance.
Nature's orchestra plays through the night,
With every chord, a soul takes flight.

The Night's Gentle Sonata

Stars twinkle softly, a lullaby clear,
Whispers of shadows, a melody near,
Moonbeams embrace the tender sky,
Crickets orchestrate the night's gentle sigh.

Feathered clouds drift, in an endless dance,
Enchanting the night with a timeless romance,
Each note of silence plays deep in the heart,
As dreams weave their magic, a delicate art.

A Tapestry of Midnight Tales

In the cloak of night, stories unfold,
Woven in whispers, secrets retold,
The stars are the pages of ages gone by,
Each twinkle a memory, each spark a sigh.

From shadows of trees, to the moon's gentle glow,
Adventures awaken in the soft winds that blow,
With every soft rustle, the twilight takes flight,
A tapestry of tales spun in the night.

Chorus of the Celestial Night

A chorus of crickets sings sweet to the stars,
Joined by the echoes of distant guitars,
The moon is the conductor, guiding the way,
Through melodies woven, in night's bright array.

Each note drifts softly, a balm for the soul,
As night wraps around, making weary hearts whole,
In cadence with breezes, the night comes alive,
With harmony flowing, where dreams may arrive.

Wandering Through Moonlit Dreams

On paths paved with silver, the wanderers roam,
Through gardens of fantasy, finding a home,
Each step is a voyage through realms undefined,
In moonlit embraces, all sorrows unwind.

Whispers of wishes ride breezes so light,
Guiding the dreams in the heart of the night,
With shadows as allies, and stars as their guide,
They wander in wonder, where magic resides.

Serenade of the Stars

Under the blanket of night,
Whispers of stars ignite.
Each twinkle a song to hear,
Dancing lights, crystal clear.

Moonbeams weave through the trees,
Carrying secrets with ease.
The cosmos hums a tune,
A serenade 'neath the moon.

Galaxies swirl in delight,
Painting the canvas of night.
In this celestial embrace,
Time slows in a timeless space.

Lost in the vastness above,
Nature's gift, purest love.
A symphony born of light,
In the calm of the night.

Chasing the Midnight Echo

Footsteps soft on the ground,
The echo whispers profound.
In the shadows, dreams take flight,
Chasing whispers of the night.

Lost among the flickering lights,
Heartbeats dance in the heights.
Time freezes, moments wane,
In pursuit of sweet refrain.

Silence wraps the world tight,
As we seek our guiding light.
Voices call from afar,
Leading us to where dreams are.

Midnight holds a promise near,
In the quiet, we persevere.
Together we'll weave our tale,
Chasing echoes on the trail.

The Lullaby of Dusk

Golden hues begin to fade,
As the sun's warm rays are laid.
Softly calling the night's embrace,
Whispers linger, time to pace.

Crickets serenade the eve,
While the world begins to weave.
Stars bloom in the indigo space,
Twinkling dreams begin to trace.

The horizon blushes deep,
As the universe starts to sleep.
Night's lullaby softly sings,
Welcoming what silence brings.

Close your eyes, drift away,
Let the twilight gently sway.
In the arms of soft night's grace,
Find your peace, a sacred place.

Velvet Skies in Blue

An ocean of blue above,
Whispers the skies of love.
Clouds drift like thoughts in flight,
Carrying dreams into the light.

Beneath this endless expanse,
We find hope in nature's dance.
Each breeze carries tales untold,
In the velvet blue, we behold.

Stars prepare for their debut,
As dusk blankets the day anew.
Embracing twilight's gentle song,
In this canvas, we belong.

Hold the moment, breathe it in,
Where the magic does begin.
Under velvet skies so true,
Life awakens, fresh as dew.

Solitude's Nocturnal Waltz

In the stillness of the night,
Stars whisper secrets bright,
Moonlight dances on the ground,
In this hush, peace is found.

Softly shadows intertwine,
Echoes of a heart divine,
Crickets sing a soft refrain,
In solitude, I feel no pain.

A gentle breeze sweeps through trees,
Carrying dreams upon the seas,
Underneath this velvet sky,
I let go of all but sighs.

Lost in thoughts that freely twirl,
In this quiet, time does curl,
Every moment, slow and grand,
In solitude, I take my stand.

The Night's Ballet of Shadows

Beneath the sky, a shadow plays,
In moonlit beams, it sways and stays,
Each movement soft, a mystic art,
The night unfolds, enchanting heart.

Whispers glide on the cool night air,
While twinkling stars begin to stare,
Through the quiet, echoes dance,
In this moment, souls entrance.

The trees in silence mark the time,
As fireflies twinkle, so sublime,
A ballet of the dark and light,
In shadows deep, the dreams take flight.

With every sweep, the night draws near,
A symphony only we can hear,
In the twilight, we take our chance,
To join the night's ethereal dance.

Gathering the Dust of Stars

We wander beneath the night,
Where constellations dance in light.
Gathering dust from distant spheres,
Whispers of ancients, dreams and fears.

Each sparkle holds a story told,
Of hearts that burned, of spirits bold.
In cosmic arms, we find our peace,
As time and space together cease.

The dust, it swirls, a gentle grace,
A tapestry in boundless space.
We reach for more, with hands outstretched,
In the universe, we feel enmeshed.

Together we embrace the glow,
Where starlit paths begin to flow.
In unity, we shine so bright,
Gathering dust of purest light.

The Horizon Drenched in Indigo

The sky spills colors, rich and deep,
As day drifts softly into sleep.
Indigo wraps the world in night,
A canvas painted with twilight light.

Waves of whispers caress the shore,
Secrets linger, forevermore.
As shadows stretch and time stands still,
The heartbeats echo, a tranquil thrill.

Stars awaken, one by one,
Dancing softly with the moon begun.
In this moment, dreams take flight,
Beneath the horizon, bathed in light.

With every breath, a tale unfolds,
Of silent wonders, love untold.
In the indigo, we find our song,
A symphony where we belong.

Echoes from the Abyss

Deep in the chasm, shadows creep,
Where secrets slumber, dark and deep.
Echoes call from the depths unknown,
Whispers of sorrow, a heart of stone.

In the silence, stories weave,
Of forgotten battles, souls that grieve.
The abyss speaks with a haunting tone,
A melody that chills to the bone.

Yet within this darkness, light may hide,
Glimmers of hope, lessons applied.
Through the echoes, we seek our way,
Guided by stars that refuse to stray.

From the depths, we rise anew,
With echoes as our guiding clue.
In the abyss, we find our might,
Emerging strong, into the light.

The Silence that Follows Dusk

When the sun dips low, the world stands still,
A hush envelops, a gentle thrill.
The silence drapes like a velvet shawl,
As nighttime whispers its ancient call.

Crickets serenade the fading light,
Each note a promise of the quiet night.
Stars emerge, guardians of dreams,
In the stillness, nothing is as it seems.

The moon ascends to take her throne,
In the silence, we're never alone.
With every heartbeat, time gently flows,
In the dark, a beauty that grows.

As shadows deepen, fears may rise,
But in the stillness, hope never dies.
We listen close as the night unfolds,
In the silence, a thousand stories told.

Solace in Celestial Shadows

In twilight's gentle grace, we roam,
Beneath the stars, we find our home.
Soft whispers call from skies above,
Wrapped in the night, we breathe of love.

The moonlight weaves a silver thread,
Guiding our hearts where dreams are led.
In shadows deep, we seek and find,
The solace cradled in the mind.

Amidst the dark, a sparkle gleams,
Echoes of long-forgotten dreams.
Together we dance on starlit shores,
Where time stands still and never pours.

With every sigh, the universe sings,
Embracing the truth that night brings.
Lost in the hush, we softly tread,
In celestial shadows, joy is spread.

Interlude of the Eclipsed Moon

When the moon bows low and hides away,
The world holds its breath in a jeweled sway.
A hush envelops the midnight scene,
In shadows deep, a magic unseen.

Stars shimmer dim under lunar shroud,
Secrets are whispered, silent yet loud.
Time drips softly like rain from the skies,
In the eclipse, truth rarely lies.

Hearts beat gently in the darkened sway,
Sweet interludes of night come to play.
Phases of light, a cosmic dance,
In the moon's embrace, we find our chance.

As darkness lifts, a glow ignites,
Awakening dreams of endless nights.
In eclipsed moments, we realize,
The beauty held in the hidden skies.

Glistening Dreams of Orion

In the expanse where stars converge,
Glistening dreams begin to surge.
Orion's bow, a tale untold,
In midnight's arms, the brave and bold.

Galaxies swirl in a cosmic dance,
Caught in the grip of fate and chance.
Celestial fires burn bright and bold,
Illuminating wonders of old.

Each twinkling star, a vision shared,
Stories of loves that have dared.
Through ages past, their light remains,
A beacon of hope in earthbound chains.

So let us gaze up, hand in hand,
To dream of futures, vast and grand.
In the grand tapestry of night's dome,
We find our legends, our true home.

Lull of the Whispering Winds

The winds carry tales through the boughs,
Soft whispers rustle, nature bows.
Gentle sighs drift through the trees,
In their embrace, we find our ease.

Every breeze brings a lullaby,
Caressing the earth, a soft goodbye.
Clouds weave hush as day departs,
In twilight's cloak, it stirs our hearts.

Dancing leaves in perfect time,
Nature's rhythm, a soothing rhyme.
With every gust, the world feels near,
In whispering winds, we lose our fear.

So close your eyes, let the winds sing,
Of ancient dreams and forgotten spring.
In nature's lull, we find our way,
As whispers guide us through the gray.

Embracing the Cosmic Silence

In the vastness where stars dwell,
Whispers of night begin to swell.
A canvas painted dark and deep,
Where secrets of the cosmos sleep.

Beyond the clamor of our days,
Silent truths in starlight blaze.
Moonlit paths, soft, gently call,
In cosmic stillness, we find all.

Treasures of the Moonlit World

Beneath the glow of silver light,
Hidden wonders come to sight.
Glistening dreams on whispered breeze,
Nature's treasures, hearts appease.

Each shadow dances, softly sways,
Enchanting realms where magic plays.
In this world of dreamy grace,
We find our peace, in quiet space.

Flickering Flames of Solace

In the hearth where embers glow,
Flickering warmth, a gentle flow.
Through the dark, a soft embrace,
In flames, we find our sacred place.

Each spark a tale, each crackle true,
Stories shared, old and new.
With every flame, our worries fade,
In solace found, hearts aren't afraid.

Twilight Gathers in the Heart

As daylight yields to evening's blend,
Twilight whispers, the day must end.
Soft colors brush the fading sky,
In stillness, our deepest thoughts lie.

With twilight's breath, we pause, we dream,
Feeling life in a gentle stream.
Gathered moments, shadows impart,
A tranquil peace, within the heart.

The Lullaby of Dusk

As day gives way to night,
The sky begins to weave,
Soft whispers in twilight's glow,
A gentle sigh to breathe.

Shadows dance on the ground,
The stars start to peep,
The world fades into silence,
Embracing rest, we sleep.

The moon sings a soothing tune,
With rays of silver light,
Crickets hum their sweet refrain,
In the arms of the night.

With every twinkling star,
Our dreams begin to rise,
The lullaby of dusk unfolds,
Underneath vast skies.

Melodies in the Midnight Veil

In the heart of midnight's cloak,
Melodies softly play,
Whispers of a haunting song,
Guide the lost astray.

The breeze carries secrets low,
As shadows twirl and sway,
A symphony of solace speaks,
In the hush of the day.

Each note a tender echo,
Spilling through the trees,
Wrapped in a velvet embrace,
Carried on the breeze.

Gently, time begins to pause,
In this tranquil scene,
Melodies in the midnight veil,
Glimmers of forgotten dreams.

Songs of the Starlit Canvas

Upon the starlit canvas bright,
Each star a tale to tell,
A chorus of the night unfolds,
In a magical spell.

The constellations dance above,
Weaving stories bold,
In the quiet of the evening,
Old legends are retold.

With every twinkle in the dark,
A whisper fills the air,
Songs of hope and wonder drift,
Beyond a world of care.

Each heartbeat in the stillness,
A rhythm strong and free,
Songs of the starlit canvas flow,
A lull to you and me.

Nocturnal Reveries

In the depths of sweet repose,
Nocturnal dreams take flight,
Where shadows weave their magic,
In the cloak of night.

Whispers of the evening breeze,
Caress the silent land,
As stars sprinkle their wishes,
Like grains of golden sand.

Lost in pools of moonlit thoughts,
Our fears begin to wane,
In every shimmering moment,
Freedom from the rain.

Nocturnal reveries gently call,
As visions start to gleam,
In the soft embrace of slumber,
We dance within our dream.

Echoes of the Darkened Heart

In shadows deep, where whispers dwell,
A heart once bright, now casts its spell.
The echoes call from deep within,
A haunting tune of loss and sin.

Through winding paths and shattered dreams,
The silent scream, a muted theme.
Yet still, a flicker dares to glow,
A spark of hope in depths of woe.

In every tear that falls like rain,
A story told of love and pain.
With every throb, the heart will yearn,
For lost embraces, life's return.

So hold the dark, embrace the night,
For dawn shall come, a guiding light.
In echoes' grip, we find our way,
To heal the heart, to face the day.

The Quietude of Evening

As daylight fades, the world grows still,
A gentle hush upon the hill.
The sun bows low, the stars take flight,
In whispers soft, the peace of night.

The trees stand tall, their silhouettes,
Embrace the calm, the night resets.
A breeze rustles leaves, a soft embrace,
In the quietude, we find our place.

Moonbeams weave through branches bare,
Illuminating dreams laid bare.
In every shadow, stories weave,
Of hopes and fears that we believe.

As night unfolds its velvet shroud,
We breathe, we sigh, away from crowd.
In tranquil moments, hearts take flight,
In the quietude of the night.

Melodies Beneath the Canopy

Beneath the boughs where shadows play,
A symphony of leaves at sway.
The rustling notes dance in the air,
A melody beyond compare.

The birds take flight, their songs so sweet,
Each feathered note, a heart's quick beat.
In harmony with nature's grace,
Life finds a way in this quiet space.

The brook hums low, a soothing tune,
Reflecting light of the silver moon.
In every ripple, stories blend,
Melodies of old, that never end.

In this embrace of green and gold,
The magic of the earth unfolds.
With every breath, the music sways,
As time stands still in sun-drenched rays.

Midnight's Gentle Breath

In midnight's hour, the world asleep,
A gentle breath, the silence deep.
Stars twinkle softly, a cosmic dance,
Whispers of dreams in sweet romance.

With every tick, the clock does chime,
In this stillness, we lose all time.
The moonlight bathes the earth in glow,
A silver thread where shadows flow.

The nightingale sings a lullaby,
As clouds drift slowly across the sky.
With every note, the heart takes flight,
In midnight's arms, we feel the night.

So close your eyes, let worries cease,
In this moment, find your peace.
In midnight's breath, we are set free,
Embracing dreams, just you and me.

Beneath the Shimmering Sky

Beneath the shimmering sky,
Whispers float on the breeze,
Dreams weave through the twilight,
Beneath the ancient trees.

Stars dance like lanterns bright,
Guiding the hearts that roam,
In the hush of the night,
They find their way back home.

Moonlight bathes the meadow,
Where shadows softly play,
Every heartbeat a echo,
In night's sweet soft array.

Beneath this cosmic veil,
Life and dreams intertwine,
In the glow of the starlight,
Our spirits rise and shine.

The Enchantment of Starlit Paths

The starlit paths are calling,
With magic in the air,
Every step, a gentle sigh,
For dreams linger everywhere.

Moonbeams kiss the flowers,
As night unfolds it's song,
In the heart of silence,
We find where we belong.

Footprints trace our stories,
In whispers soft and low,
Guided by the shimmer,
Of stars that gently glow.

In this enchanting moment,
Time feels like a dream,
Underneath the canvas,
Of the night's brilliant gleam.

Surrender to the Night

Surrender to the night,
Where shadows softly blend,
In the arms of silence,
We find our hearts can mend.

Stars spin tales of longing,
In the cloak of dusk's embrace,
Each twinkle a soft promise,
That time shall leave no trace.

Close your eyes to the chaos,
Let the world drift away,
In the stillness we're anchored,
'Til the break of day.

Surrender to the beauty,
Of the dark's gentle sigh,
In the realm of night's wonders,
Our spirits learn to fly.

Threads of Night's Tapestry

Threads of night's tapestry,
Are woven with the stars,
Each shimmer tells a story,
Of dreams from near and far.

In the loom of the heavens,
Fate dances on a thread,
Every heartbeat, a color,
In the fabric of the dead.

Moonlight glints like diamonds,
Adorning what we know,
Binding moments and memories,
In the velvet night's flow.

As dawn begins its whisper,
We cherish every hue,
Threads of night's tapestry,
Guide our souls anew.

Reverberations at Dusk

Whispers linger in the air,
As day gives way to night.
Shadows dance without a care,
In fading echoes, lost to light.

The horizon bleeds with gold,
As silence finds its wings.
Secrets of the dark unfold,
While twilight softly sings.

Each star a distant call,
A promise yet unmade.
In the stillness, we feel small,
By reverberations laid.

Embrace the dusk's sweet grace,
As night takes gentle hold.
In this sacred, quiet space,
Our dreams in shadows told.

Secrets of the Lunar Tides

Beneath the moon's soft gaze,
The ocean hums a tune.
Whispers weave through night's haze,
Secrets kept by the moon.

Waves that swell and recede,
Unfold the stories deep.
In the night's gentle plead,
The tides their secrets keep.

Dancing to the lunar pull,
Each ripple finds its way.
Nature's heart, a wondrous lull,
In silver beams, they sway.

Underneath this glowing orb,
Mysterious and bright.
The ocean's soul absorbs,
The calm of night's delight.

Hymn of the Sable Skies

In the cloak of night's embrace,
Stars ignite a cosmic song.
Beneath the vast, eternal space,
The heartbeats feel so strong.

Whispers of the ancient past,
Drift through the stellar streams.
In moments fleeting, yet so fast,
We chase our quiet dreams.

Each constellation sings a note,
In harmony with time.
From birth to death, we all float,
In rhythms and in rhyme.

The sable skies, our sacred site,
Where wishes dare to fly.
In the depth of starry night,
We find our reason why.

Evening's Embrace

Crimson hues drape the land,
As day folds into night.
Gentle breezes softly grand,
Wrap the world in twilight.

The sounds of evening sigh,
With whispers soft and low.
As shadows start to fly,
The stars begin to glow.

In the arms of fading light,
We gather hopes anew.
Every moment, pure delight,
As dreams come into view.

So let us cherish this time,
Where day and night entwine.
In evening's warm and tender rhyme,
Our hearts forever shine.

The Lure of the Ebon Horizon

In the shadowed depths of night,
Ebon waves sway and sigh,
Stars glimmer like lost dreams,
Calling souls to fly.

Whispers ebb on the tide,
Secrets held so tight,
The horizon beckons gently,
A dance of dark and light.

Mysteries in silence churn,
As shadows seek their place,
Underneath the vast expanse,
Of eternity's embrace.

Beneath the veil of night,
Lies a world untold,
Where the heart finds its compass,
And the brave become bold.

Echoes of the Midnight Breeze

Whispers carry through the trees,
Soft like a lover's sigh,
Echoes dance in the cool air,
Beneath a velvet sky.

The moon spills secrets bright,
On a path of silver light,
Guiding wanderers onward,
Through the tranquil night.

Leaves rustle with a song,
Of stories long gone by,
The midnight breeze remembers,
Each breath, each goodbye.

In the stillness, hearts align,
With nature's gentle grace,
As echoes of the moment,
Fill the empty space.

Moonlit Whispers

Beneath the moon's soft gaze,
Whispers float like mist,
Secrets held in shadows,
In darkness, love persists.

Cool light caresses dreams,
As night unveils its art,
Painting wishes on the sky,
Filling every heart.

Stars blink in knowing joy,
A symphony of night,
Where velvet soft confessions,
Spark like fireflies' flight.

In the hush of midnight,
Every soul finds its tune,
Dancing with the silence,
Underneath the moon.

Shadows of Twilight

As daylight bids farewell,
Shadows stretch and grow,
A canvas brushed in purple,
With the sun's final glow.

Whispers of the night rise,
As stars begin their dance,
Twilight wraps the world softly,
In a sweet, timeless trance.

The horizon cradles dreams,
In the hues of fading light,
While shadows tell their stories,
Of the coming night.

In the gentle twilight's hand,
All secrets find their way,
Embracing the unknown,
At the end of day.

Harmonies in the Underbelly of Darkness

In shadows deep, soft whispers weave,
Echoes of secrets the night believes.
A dance of silence, a tranquil sigh,
Where fears dissolve and dreams can fly.

Beneath the veil, where silence reigns,
Murmurs of hope in gentle strains.
The heartbeats thrum, a cryptic song,
Entwined in night where we belong.

Stars sprinkle light on hidden fears,
Each glimmering spark dries whispered tears.
In the dark, we find our way,
Through melodies that softly play.

As shadows meld into the light,
We dance in dreams, through endless night.
With every note, we learn to see,
The harmonies of what may be.

The Crescendo of Evening Dreams

Twilight blends with velvet skies,
Whispers of dusk begin to rise.
Petals of dreams in soft embrace,
Painting hope in a tranquil space.

The horizon glows, a fading tune,
Light dims gently, surrendering soon.
In the stillness, our hearts align,
A symphony played by stars that shine.

The wind carries secrets from afar,
Echoing wishes with each twinkling star.
In this moment, time stands still,
As dreams awaken, a quiet thrill.

With every breath, a crescendo swells,
Tales of the night that time compels.
Together we weave, a tapestry bright,
In the heart of our evening flight.

Nightfall's Silent Sonnet

As shadows cloak the fading light,
Day surrenders to the night.
With whispers soft, the stars ignite,
A silent sonnet of pure delight.

Moonbeams dance on curtains drawn,
Painting dreams of a new dawn.
In the hush, secrets unfold,
In gentle strokes, our stories told.

Pause a moment, breathe it in,
The stillness where magic begins.
In echoes low, our hopes take flight,
Within the heart of velvet night.

Each twinkling star, a verse in rhyme,
A melody woven in space and time.
With open hearts, we listen close,
To the silent sonnet that night chose.

A Symphony of Hidden Light

In the depth of night, where shadows play,
A symphony stirs, guiding our way.
Notes wrapped in dreams, soft as a sigh,
In the stillness of night, we learn to fly.

With whispered tunes that brush the air,
Each hidden light, a secret shared.
Against the dark, our spirits rise,
In a dance of shadows and starlit skies.

The world awaits with bated breath,
In melodies born from what feels like death.
Yet through the dark, we find our song,
Resonating deep where we belong.

A tapestry woven with threads of night,
In every flicker, a glimpse of light.
Together we roam, hearts intertwined,
In a symphony that transcends time.

The Veil of Night's Embrace

In shadows deep, where silence sighs,
The stars awake, bright in the skies.
Whispers float on the cool, soft breeze,
A dance of dreams beneath the trees.

The moon drapes light on fields of grey,
As twilight slowly fades away.
Wrapped in the cloak of twilight's song,
The night unfolds, where we belong.

Silhouettes twirl in a gentle haze,
Lost in the magic of hidden ways.
The world seems still, a secret kept,
In night's embrace, the heart has leapt.

So linger here, where shadows play,
Let worries melt and drift away.
For in the dark, new paths ignite,
In the veils of night, we find our light.

Secrets of the Nocturnal Garden

Under the gaze of a silver moon,
Petals whisper, a soft-spun tune.
In fragrant shadows, secrets sigh,
Where starlit blossoms dare to lie.

The crickets chirp their midnight song,
In hidden corners where dreams belong.
Each bloom a tale, a whispered word,
In this garden where hopes are heard.

A lantern glows in the gentle night,
Guiding hearts with its tender light.
The secrets held in nature's bower,
Awake a magic, a hidden power.

As night unfolds its velvet cloak,
In the garden, love's fire evokes.
Embrace the hush, and listen close,
For in the dark, the heart can chose.

Echoed Lullabies from the Abyss

In the deep, where shadows weave,
Lullabies of the lost believe.
Echoes dance in the velvet dark,
Whispers ride on the ocean's lark.

Crashing waves bring forth the dreams,
As the moonlight spills in silver streams.
Memories drift on a ghostly tide,
In the abyss, where secrets hide.

Softly cradled in sleep's embrace,
Time slows down in this sacred space.
A symphony played on the starry sea,
Calling forth realms where the heart can be free.

So let the echoes tenderly guide,
Through hidden currents, gently slide.
In the depths, feel the lullabies soar,
For in the abyss, we are forevermore.

The Call of the Darkening Sky

When the sun retreats, and shadows spread,
The call of night drapes over the bed.
Stars begin their silent flight,
Whispering secrets in the dimming light.

Thunder rumbles through the vast expanse,
As the moon prepares for its evening dance.
With every heartbeat, the world slows down,
In the twilight's grip, where dreams are found.

The sky unveils its starry attire,
Lighting the heart with a curious fire.
Within the stillness, the wild winds sigh,
Awakening spirits beneath the sky.

So heed the call, and softly tread,
Where night's enchantments softly spread.
In the darkening canvas, let us reply,
To the whispers woven in the twilight sigh.

Reflections in Starlit Waters

In the calm of evening's glow,
Rippling dreams begin to flow.
Stars above, they softly gleam,
Whispers caught in a silver stream.

Moonlight dances on the lake,
Echoes of a night awake.
Crickets sing their twilight song,
To the night, we all belong.

Reflections bloom in twilight's haze,
Memories of the fading days.
Gently weaving tales of old,
In the water, secrets unfold.

Time, a river flowing bright,
Cradles dreams in velvet night.
We find peace in the serene,
In starlit waters, hope is seen.

Dreaming Beneath the Moon

In a world where shadows play,
Dreams are sown at the end of day.
Beneath the moon's embrace so light,
Our hopes take wing and take to flight.

Stars are but the night's soft breath,
Breathing life where silence met.
Wishes whispered on a breeze,
Float like petals from the trees.

Close your eyes, let visions start,
Feel the rhythm of your heart.
In this magic, find your tune,
Together, dreaming 'neath the moon.

Time drifts by in gentle sways,
Crafting dreams in myriad ways.
Each heartbeat, a promise held tight,
As we dance in the velvet night.

Nightfall's Gentle Embrace

Nightfall brings a soft embrace,
Wrapping dreams in silent space.
Dusk unfolds, a shroud of peace,
As the day begins to cease.

Gentle whispers fill the air,
While shadows linger everywhere.
Underneath the silver gleam,
We're embraced in twilight's dream.

Stars appear like scattered seeds,
Nurturing our heart's deep needs.
With each twinkle, tales are spun,
Binding us till night is done.

In the moment, time stands still,
As we drink from night's soft will.
In this hush, our fears erase,
Finding solace in nightfall's grace.

Songs of the Silver Horizon

At dawn's edge, the silver sea,
Whispers songs of prophecy.
Waves that dance in morning's light,
Carry dreams from endless night.

Seagulls cry a melody,
Chasing shadows wild and free.
In the distance, echoes call,
Songs that rise and softly fall.

The horizon, a canvas wide,
Painted with the ocean's tide.
Colors merge, a soft embrace,
Nature's heart in vibrant grace.

Listen close, the world will sing,
Of the secrets that mornings bring.
Onward through the dawn we glide,
Together, 'neath the rising tide.

Whispers of the Moonlit Hours

In the hush of night, secrets float,
Moonbeams dance, on dreams they gloat,
Silvan shades in a gentle sway,
Whispers beckon, come take your stay.

Stars peek down through the velvet sky,
Softly casting their twinkling sigh,
Each breath a tale, each glance a spark,
In the realm of shadows, we leave our mark.

Branches sway in a haunting tune,
Lost in the lullaby of the moon,
Every flicker, every sigh,
Guides our hearts as the night drifts by.

Let the silence cradle our hopes,
In the depths where the starlight gropes,
Under the veil of a midnight owl,
Whispers envelop, a soothing prowl.

Serenade of Shadows

In the twilight's soft embrace,
Shadows waltz, a ghostly chase,
Fingers of mist weave through the trees,
As whispers dance upon the breeze.

Crickets sing their evening song,
Time holds still, where dreams belong,
Moonlit paths, where phantoms play,
Serenading night to welcome day.

Lightly tread where soft hearts sigh,
With every shadow, worlds drift by,
In the echoes of the night's caress,
We find solace, we find our rest.

A melody spun in the dark,
Hope ignites, with each small spark,
Underneath the stars' bright glow,
A serenade of shadows flows.

A Ballad Beneath the Stars

Beneath the sky where dreams abide,
A ballad calls, a gentle tide,
Voices blend in the cool night air,
Stories linger, woven with care.

Each star a note in the cosmic song,
Crafting memories where we belong,
Wandering souls, lost and free,
Harmonizing with eternity.

Glimmers of hope in the deepened blue,
A rhythm whispers, guiding us through,
As shadows play on the silver grass,
Moments captured, too sweet to pass.

In the dance of night, hearts entwine,
While the universe spins, so divine,
With every heartbeat, the verses unfold,
A ballad cherished, a tale retold.

Echoes Amidst the Twilight

Amidst the twilight, echoes ring,
A soft refrain the night does sing,
Fading light as colors blend,
In whispered tones, dreams ascend.

Horizon draped in shades of grey,
As daylight bows to night's ballet,
Every shadow stretched and lean,
Painting stories, vivid and keen.

Stars emerge with a steadfast grace,
Glimpses of light in a quiet space,
As silence deepens, hearts align,
In the echoes, we entwine.

In twilight's hold, we find our place,
With every breath, a memory traced,
Let time pause in this gentle glow,
As echoes linger, soft and slow.

Celestial Jazz of Twilight

In twilight's glow, the stars awaken,
Soft whispers dance, the night unshaken.
The cosmos plays a sultry tune,
As crickets serenade the moon.

Light and shadow, they intertwine,
Melodies flow like aged red wine.
Each note a brushstroke on the night,
Painting dreams in silver light.

Constellations sway with grace,
In this symphony, we find our place.
A canvas vast, the universe wide,
In celestial jazz, we find our guide.

So linger here as night unfolds,
In the harmony of dusk, stories told.
Let the world fade with the sun's last breath,
In twilight's arms, we dance with death.

Luminous Shadows

Shadows stretch in the softest light,
Glowing edges define the night.
Figures dance where unknowns meet,
In the silence, secrets greet.

Flickering lamps cast gentle glow,
Illuminating what we don't know.
In the dark, our thoughts take flight,
Painting worlds in the absence of sight.

Every corner holds a forgotten tale,
Wrapped in hopes, hidden like a veil.
Luminous whispers beckon us near,
In the shadows, we confront our fear.

Vibrant contrasts of dark and bright,
Life's dance unfolds, a wondrous sight.
In luminous shadows, we find our way,
Embracing the night, come what may.

Flickers of Memory in Darkness

In the dark, memories flare,
Flickers haunting, a whispered prayer.
Fragments of laughter dance in the air,
Soft echoes linger, a gentle snare.

Time stretches thin, like a fragile thread,
Woven tightly with words unsaid.
Images pulse in the quiet night,
Painting the past in subdued light.

Each moment a spark, each thought a glow,
In the shadows, our feelings flow.
Glimmers of joy, hints of despair,
We gather the pieces, woven with care.

As darkness wraps around our hearts,
We find solace in memory's arts.
Flickers ignite in the stillness we face,
A tapestry woven, time's sweet embrace.

Fables Beneath Twilight's Gaze

Beneath twilight's gaze, tales unfold,
Whispers of adventures yet untold.
Leaves rustle softly in the breeze,
Each story beckons, begging to please.

Creatures linger in fading light,
Guardians of secrets, holding tight.
In their eyes, wisdom shines bright,
Echoes of fables seeking insight.

The moon cradles stories from afar,
Guiding lost souls, like a distant star.
In this twilight realm, magic is born,
From every shadow, a new world is worn.

So pause and listen, let nature speak,
In twilight's embrace, we are all unique.
Fables unfold as night draws near,
In the heart of the dusk, we find no fear.

The Chorus of Dusk's Breath

As shadows stretch, the day departs,
The evening sighs in gentle arts.
A palette of hues begins to blend,
In twilight's arms, our spirits mend.

The air grows cool, a whispered note,
On silent winds, our dreams will float.
Each star ignites a tale to share,
The night awaits beneath its care.

Moonlight dances on serene lakes,
A symphony of soft heartaches.
With every breath, the world unwinds,
In dusk's embrace, our solace finds.

Let echoes of the evening ring,
In harmony, the darkness sings.
Together bound in night's caress,
In every heart, we find our rest.

Whispers in the Gloom

In shadows deep, where secrets dwell,
The night conceals its haunting spell.
A rustle soft, a fleeting shade,
In whispered tones, our fears cascade.

The rhythm of the midnight breeze,
Carries tales from ancient trees.
Each rustling leaf a ghostly sigh,
In the gloom, our worries fly.

The moon, a guardian up above,
Watches over with gentle love.
In veils of night, our hopes renew,
Embracing dreams both old and new.

So listen close to what they say,
In whispers lost, they guide our way.
Each moment holds a spark divine,
In shadows dark, our spirits shine.

The Melody of Midnight's Kiss

When the clock strikes, the world stands still,
In quiet hearts, a longing thrill.
A serenade beneath the stars,
Where every note our essence jars.

The night unfolds its velvet sheet,
In every heartbeat, time must meet.
A tender gaze, a fleeting touch,
In midnight's arms, we feel so much.

Each whisper soft, a gentle sway,
Awakens dreams that dance and play.
In secret moments, shadows play,
The music guides, we find our way.

An echo of a love once lost,
In melodies, we find the cost.
Yet through the pain, a beauty grows,
In midnight's kiss, our hearts compose.

Twilight's Euphony

As day gives way to night's embrace,
The sky adorns a whispered grace.
In colors bold, the sun descends,
An euphony that never ends.

The horizon blushes, stars align,
In this retreat, our dreams entwine.
Each moment sings a fleeting tune,
In twilight's glow, we find our boon.

The breath of dusk, a tranquil balm,
In gentle hues, we find our calm.
With every note the world can play,
A symphony of dreams at bay.

So let us linger in this hour,
Embrace the night and feel its power.
In twilight's euphony, we'll soar,
Forever bound to dream once more.

The Ballad of Dreaming Souls

In shadows deep, the whispers sigh,
A dance of spirits, you and I.
Through twilight's veil, our wishes soar,
On wings of hope, forevermore.

Beneath the stars, our secrets share,
In the stillness, a gentle prayer.
Awake we dream, and dream we strive,
Together here, our souls alive.

With every heartbeat, stories weave,
In realms of night, we learn to believe.
Embrace the light, let visions shine,
For in our dreams, the world aligns.

So let us roam, through night and gloom,
With every spark, dispel the doom.
In dreams we find, our truest fate,
Together strong, we resonate.

Starlit Serenade

Underneath a vast, velvet sky,
Stars twinkle softly, like a sigh.
In quiet moments, hearts entwine,
A melody sweet, our souls align.

Whispers of night, a gentle breeze,
Rustle through leaves, with effortless ease.
The moonlight bathes the earth anew,
While we dance on dreams, just me and you.

With every note, the world stands still,
As nature harmonizes at will.
A serenade, through shadows cast,
Unlocks our hearts, as moments pass.

In this lullaby, our spirits soar,
A starlit dance, forevermore.
With every shimmer, the night invites,
A promise kept in endless nights.

Twilight's Gentle Aria

As day gives in to night's embrace,
Twilight sings in colors' grace.
A tranquil hush, the world awaits,
With dreams that dance at evening's gates.

Soft hues blend in the fading light,
A symphony of day to night.
Whispers weave through the cool, calm air,
In this stillness, we find our prayer.

The stars emerge, like notes on sheets,
As twilight hums, the silence greets.
In every breath, the magic swells,
An aria only twilight tells.

So pause awhile, let worries cease,
In twilight's arms, we find our peace.
With every note our hearts compose,
In gentle twilight, love's secret grows.

Echoing through the Silence of Darkness

In shadowed depths where whispers dwell,
Echoes linger, a timeless spell.
Through silence thick, our voices call,
Resonate in the heart of all.

With every pulse, the shadows sway,
A haunting tune, in disarray.
Yet through the dark, a light does gleam,
Guiding us closer, to hope we cling.

In depths unknown, we find our way,
Through quiet paths, we dare to stay.
In echoes deep, we shape our fate,
For even darkness can illuminate.

So hear the song that calls us near,
Through every echo, dispel the fear.
For in the silence, strength we find,
In darkest nights, our hearts aligned.

Revelations at Midnight

In shadows deep where secrets dwell,
The clock strikes twelve, a distant bell.
Whispers dance on velvet air,
Unfolding truths, laid bare and rare.

Moonlight spills on silent streets,
A tender heart with racing beats.
In every corner, dreams ignite,
As souls embrace the deepest night.

Figures glide through dusky haze,
Casting light on hidden ways.
With every breath, a story spins,
In midnight's clutch, where hope begins.

The stars conspire, a cosmic plan,
Each twinkle born from love's sweet span.
With every shadow, something new,
Revelations bloom, in midnight's hue.

The Softest Shade of Evening

The sun melts down, a golden sphere,
Whispers of dusk, a gentle cheer.
Clouds blushing pink, they float so light,
Embracing the warmth of coming night.

Crickets sing their serenade,
As twilight's veil begins to fade.
Softly now, the world unwinds,
In evening's arms, solace finds.

Stars peek out from their hidden beds,
Painting the sky with silver threads.
Breezes carry scents of rest,
A tender heart feels truly blessed.

The night stretches, a canvas wide,
In its embrace, dreams will reside.
Each moment savored, softly swayed,
In the softest shade, love is laid.

Nocturne of the Unseen

In the stillness where shadows creep,
Whispers gather, secrets keep.
A nocturne played on silent strings,
The magic of night, the heart it brings.

Underneath a velvet dome,
The unseen spirits find their home.
With every rustle, the world awakes,
In midnight's grasp, the silence breaks.

Stars are guides for wandering souls,
Charting paths to distant goals.
In darkness, beauty finds its voice,
A lullaby, a gentle choice.

As time drifts by, the world stands still,
The unseen dance beneath the will.
Through moonlit dreams, our hearts will soar,
In nocturne's grace, forevermore.

Ballad of the Wandering Star

A star once bright, it lost its way,
Drifting through night, it yearned to stay.
Tales of journeys, brave and far,
It sings the ballad of the wandering star.

Through cosmic seas, it sails alone,
Across the skies, its light has shone.
With every heartbeat, a wish is made,
By dreamers lost in the stars' cascade.

From dawn till dusk, it paints the night,
Guiding hearts in its steadfast light.
With every glance, we find our place,
In the ballad sung through endless space.

Oh, how it dances, a glittering spark,
In the deep canvas, forever stark.
The wandering star will ever roam,
In its bright glow, we find our home.

The Nocturne of Forgotten Stars

Once they shone bright, now they fade,
Whispers of light in the dark parade.
Silent echoes of a bright past,
Fading memories, shadows cast.

In the velvet sky, they weave and wane,
Tales untold of joy and pain.
Stars that were dreamt, now just dust,
Lost among time, forgotten trust.

Their glimmer calls to the hearts of few,
Wishing for light in a world so blue.
Gone are the dreams that once seemed near,
In the nocturne, we hold our fears.

Yet in their absence, new ones will rise,
Guided by hope, beneath endless skies.
So we gaze up, with wonder anew,
In the dark night, the brightness grew.

Driftwood Dreams

On the shore where tides embrace,
Driftwood dreams find their place.
Whispers of waves in the breeze,
Carried afar like forgotten pleas.

Each piece a story, weathered and worn,
Silent witness to hope reborn.
The sun sets low, painting the sand,
Driftwood whispers of a far-off land.

Beneath the moon's soft, silver light,
They dance and shimmer, taking flight.
Dreams once lost, now drift ashore,
Echoes of life, forevermore.

In this haven, we find our muse,
Among the wood, we shall not lose.
Each wave a promise, each tide a scheme,
In the quiet night, we weave a dream.

Shadows that Brew

In the corners where whispers creep,
Shadows that brew, secrets to keep.
Lurking softly in the night's embrace,
Time stands still in this darkened space.

Ghostly forms in flickering light,
Dancing shadows in the dead of night.
Each flicker tells a tale untold,
Of dreams and fears, of hearts grown cold.

Beneath the surface, the darkness hums,
A symphony of all that comes.
Through the dark, they play and roam,
In the shadows, we find our home.

With every thrum, we start to see,
The beauty in shadows, wild and free.
In the silence, truths we glean,
In shadows that brew, we find our dream.

A Songcarved in Starlight

In the quiet night, a melody sighs,
A songcarved in starlight, where magic lies.
Notes weave through the air like a silken thread,
Softly whispering what must be said.

Each star a note, bright on the page,
A timeless symphony, love and rage.
Harmony dances in the glow above,
A cosmic tune of lost and found love.

Dreams take flight on the wings of night,
Carved in starlight, pure and bright.
With each heartbeat, the rhythm flows,
A song of the universe, ever it grows.

Listen closely to the starlit song,
In its embrace, we all belong.
With every twinkle, let your spirit soar,
In the night's embrace, we seek for more.

Celestial Reverie

In the hush of night, stars gleam bright,
Whispers of dreams take graceful flight.
Silver clouds drift, soft and slow,
Echoes of hopes, in shadows they flow.

Galaxies dance in endless grace,
Each twinkle a story, a memory's trace.
Moonlit secrets shared with the wind,
A celestial tapestry, where dreams begin.

Hearts entwined under the darkened sky,
Love's gentle sigh, a soft lullaby.
Waves of stardust in tender embrace,
Time suspends in this magical space.

Endless wonder painted in night,
Softly we drift in the surreal light.
Awash with the beauty, our spirits soar,
In the realm of dreams, forevermore.

Burning Embers Under Moonlight

Flickering flames in the cool night air,
A circle of warmth, free from despair.
Whispering secrets in glowing tones,
Beneath the watchful moon, our hearts find homes.

Embers rise, casting shadows long,
In the dance of night, we feel so strong.
The world fades away, just us alone,
In the fire's glow, we have truly grown.

Stories shared in the glow so warm,
Laughter like sparks, a comforting charm.
Later, the embers begin to wane,
Yet memories linger, like gentle rain.

As the night deepens, we hold each tight,
Our souls ignite with a shared delight.
In the flame's embrace, we find our way,
Burning embers light the paths we sway.

Stardust and Solitude

Lost in the stillness, the night draws near,
Whispers of stardust, soft and clear.
Lonely hearts wander, searching for light,
In solitude's grasp, we find our flight.

Dreams in the quiet rise like the mist,
Each flicker of hope, gently kissed.
Under the vastness, our fears cast away,
Embracing the silence, we learn to stay.

A canvas of starshine brushes the night,
Painting our sorrows in shades of light.
Each trail of stardust, a path to find,
In solitude's embrace, we're redefined.

Connected by silence, we find our voice,
In the heart of the night, we make our choice.
To dance with the shadows, to bask in the glow,
In stardust and solitude, together we grow.

Reverberations of the Gloom

In the depths of silence, darkness speaks,
Echoes of sorrows, the heartache peaks.
Shadows linger where light can't tread,
Whispers of pain in the words unsaid.

Moonlight weeps for a world unseen,
Veils of shadow cloaked in between.
Yet in the quiet, resilience blooms,
Like flowers awakened amidst the gloom.

Each pulse in the night holds a story untold,
Fleeting moments, the brave and the bold.
Traces of hope in the night's icy breath,
Woven in whispers of love and of death.

Though reverberations of gloom may surround,
Beneath it all, a new strength is found.
In the dark's embrace, we rise and endure,
From shadows we learn, our hearts make us pure.

The Dance of the Fireflies

In twilight's glow, they flit and swirl,
A ballet of lights, a silver pearl.
Amidst the grass, they weave and play,
A gentle whisper at close of day.

With every spark, a story told,
Of summer evenings, warm and bold.
They twinkle bright, a fleeting theme,
A dance of light, a soft dream.

Beneath the stars, they find their way,
A flickering guide, as night holds sway.
In their soft glow, we find delight,
A tranquil heart beneath the night.

So let us gaze and lose our cares,
In rhythmic flight of lantern's flares.
Together here, where shadows blend,
The dance of dreams that never end.

Secrets Carried on the Breeze

Whispers float on gentle air,
Echoes of tales hidden with care.
Leaves rustle soft, the world takes heed,
A breeze carries every unspoken need.

Through valleys deep and mountains high,
The secrets drift, as time slips by.
In every sigh, a longing breath,
Stories of life, love's dance, and death.

As sunlight fades, shadows emerge,
The breeze awakens, tales converge.
A fleeting thought, a moment lost,
In every whisper, we count the cost.

So listen close, with heart and mind,
For in the wind, such truths you'll find.
Each secret carried, a tale to weave,
In the soft sighs of those who believe.

Whispers of the Cosmic Veil

Stars adorn the velvet night,
Lost in dreams, we take flight.
Across the dark, a cosmic stream,
Whispers weave through each shared dream.

Galaxies twirl, celestial grace,
In silent realms, we find our place.
Each twinkle tells a story grand,
Of time and space, of life so planned.

Through the void, our voices blend,
To the cosmos, our hearts we send.
In whispers soft, we feel alive,
Among the stars, our spirits thrive.

So lean into the night's embrace,
Find solace in the universe's face.
For in the silence, love reveals,
The whispers shared through cosmic veils.

A Canvas of Darkened Dreams

In shadows cast by whispered night,
A canvas waits, devoid of light.
Brush strokes of silence, deep and vast,
Echoes of futures, present, past.

With every hue, a heart laid bare,
In strokes of sorrow, strokes of care.
Colors blend, then fade away,
A tapestry spun from dreams that sway.

The palette shifts, from dark to bright,
In every tear, in every plight.
Yet beauty glows beneath the seam,
A hidden light in darkened dreams.

So paint your thoughts upon the night,
Each dream a star, each hope a light.
For in this canvas, spirits gleam,
The artistry of life's vast dream.

The Nightingale's Soliloquy

In the quiet of the night,
A song floats on the breeze,
Softly weaving through the trees,
The nightingale takes flight.

Whispers of dreams unfold,
In shadows, tales are spun,
A melody has begun,
With secrets it has told.

Underneath the silver stars,
It sings of love and loss,
Each note a gentle gloss,
A serenade from afar.

In the depth of moonlit hours,
The world stands still to hear,
The nightingale draws near,
Embracing night's sweet powers.

Twilight's Embrace

As the sun begins to wane,
Colors blend in soft delight,
Embers of the day take flight,
In twilight's calm refrain.

Shadows stretch and gently creep,
Daylight bows to night's allure,
In the dusk, hearts feel secure,
Time slows down, we softly weep.

Sky painted with hues of gold,
A canvas vast and deep,
In silence, the world will sleep,
As evening's arms unfold.

Moments linger, soft and sweet,
Underneath the fading light,
In dusk, we find our sight,
In twilight's warm heartbeat.

Tides of Dusk

The ocean whispers to the shore,
As daylight bids its soft goodbye,
A golden hue spills from the sky,
In waves that dance and gently roar.

Seabirds call with voices low,
The twilight lingers in the air,
In the quiet, there's a prayer,
As the tides begin to flow.

Stars emerge in twilight's grace,
Each one a beacon, shining bright,
Guiding sailors through the night,
As darkness carves a sacred space.

The horizon fades to deep blue,
Where dreams and whispers intertwine,
In the night's embrace, so fine,
The tides of dusk hold true.

The Lanterns of the Soul

Each heart holds a glowing light,
A lantern flickers in the dark,
With every spark, a timeless mark,
Guiding dreams through endless night.

In shadows deep, they gently sway,
Whispering tales of joy and woe,
In their glow, we come to know,
The beauty found in every day.

Through storms that rattle, winds that howl,
These lights remain, steadfast and bright,
Burning fiercely in the night,
The lanterns of the wandering soul.

Together they dance, they shine, they weave,
A tapestry of hope and grace,
In the heart's sacred space,
A reminder to love and believe.

Caress of the Night's Veil

The moon hangs low, a silver grace,
Whispers of dreams in the shadowed space.
Gentle breezes carry secrets near,
Night's soft caress, a soothing hear.

Stars flicker like lanterns in the dark,
Illuminating paths with a soft spark.
Crickets sing in a quiet refrain,
Nature's lullaby, a sweet refrain.

Trees sway slowly, a dance of peace,
In the cool embrace, all troubles cease.
Darkness wraps like a velvet shroud,
Within its arms, we dream aloud.

As night unfolds, the world unveils,
In the hush of time, where magic dwells.
Wrapped in silence, we find our way,
Until dawn breaks, heralding day.

Hues of the Northern Night

In the northern sky, colors collide,
A palette of emerald, deep navy tide.
Auroras dance, a shimmering flow,
Painting the night with a radiant glow.

Beneath the stars, the cold winds blow,
Each gust a whisper, secrets to sow.
Silhouettes wander through frosted trees,
Engulfed in the magic, carried by breeze.

Mountains stand tall, draped in white,
Guardians of dreams in the shimmering night.
Nature's canvas, bold and bright,
The northern lights, a breathtaking sight.

In this realm where silence reigns,
Hearts are bound, freed from all chains.
Hues of the night, forever in flight,
In the northern embrace, we find our light.

Awakened Whispers of Solitude

In solitude's arms, the heart reveals,
Softened truths, where silence heals.
Gentle thoughts flutter like leaves,
Whispers of solace that the mind weaves.

Alone, yet not lost, in the stillness found,
Echoes of clarity, profound and sound.
Each moment savored, a breath of ease,
A tranquil dance in the evening breeze.

Stars weave stories in the pitch-black sky,
Encouraging hearts to fear not, but fly.
In the quiet, we learn to see,
The beauty of being, just you and me.

Awakened whispers, softly they call,
Inviting the spirit to rise, not to fall.
In solitude's grace, our souls align,
Finding treasures, in silence divine.

Stars that Whisper

Stars that whisper in the night sky,
Silent tales as they twinkle high.
Each shimmer a message, a secret kept,
Guardians of dreams in the dark, they've wept.

In the stillness, their voices sing,
A cosmic choir, through voids they bring.
Celestial myths from ages past,
Filling the heart with the shadows cast.

Beneath their glow, the world feels new,
A blanket of hope, a shimmering dew.
With every glance at their distant light,
We weave our wishes into the night.

Stars that whisper, guiding our ways,
In their presence, we find courage to stay.
A tapestry woven of dreams and flight,
In the vast expanse of the endless night.

9 789916 905531